Southern
Oregon
Antiques &
Collectibles
Club

This Book Is A Gift To The
Jackson County Library System
from

Southern Oregon
Antiques and
Collectibles Club

ABC
PLATES
&
MUGS

IDENTIFICATION AND VALUE GUIDE

IRENE
&
RALPH
LINDSAY

JACKSON COUNTY
LIBRARY SERVICES
MEDFORD, OR 97501

Searching For A Publisher?

We are always looking for knowledgeable people considered to be experts within their fields. If you feel that there is a real need for a book on your collectible subject and have a large comprehensive collection, contact Collector Books.

Front cover: Shown are ABC plates, mugs, and a cup pictured in this book: Peter Rabbit (litho tin), two English soft paste plates (Staffordshire), two English mugs, and a German cup and plate (hard paste).

Cover design by: Beth Summers
Book design by: Mary Ann Dorris

Additional copies of this book may be ordered from:

COLLECTOR BOOKS
P.O. Box 3009
Paducah, Kentucky 42002-3009

@$24.95. Add $2.00 for postage and handling.

❧CONTENTS❧

❧ *ACKNOWLEDGMENTS* ❧

Our sincere thanks to the following people for their help in the production of this book. Auctioneer and antiques dealer Jim Frey and Mrs. Frey; Donna and Bill Gray, Columbia, MD, Harker Pottery authorities; Dr. Anne Lindsay Weiss, Victorian England and Dickens authority; J. Dean Austin and Tom Russell, cover photography. And for her assistance above and beyond, Dr. Joan M. George.

The Chalalas, Millie and Joe, about 1965. The premier collectors of ABC china.

Irene knew both Millie and Joe and appreciated their assistance and friendship as she began her collection. After Joe passed on, I made the acquaintance of Millie, cementing our relationship by sending her cat, Saucy, catnip from the patch behind our barn.

Irene and I visited Millie a few times at her Willow Street, PA, home and came to know her well. As her illness progressed she found it necessary to sell her huge collection, and Irene attended both of her public sales. Many of the plates and mugs in this book are from the Chalala collection.

Irene Lindsay and Millie Chalala, 1989.

ABC Collector's Circle

This quarterly publication is published by New Jersey educator, Dr. Joan M. George. Dr. George saw a need for a newsletter for the purpose of gathering information and sharing experiences and knowledge in the field of ABC plates and mugs.

Sixteen pages at present, the *ABC Collector's Circle* consists of an "Our Readers Write" column, in which individual subscribers describe their collections, favorites, and wants; reprints of articles on ABC china; types of ABC ware such as Kate Greenaway and Campbell Kids; etc.

Some of the members have ABC plates for sale, with conditions and prices. Resource materials and current auction prices are also featured.

Published four times a year, $25 U.S. and Canada, $30 other. Please make U.S. checks out to Joan George. All other funds in U.S. money orders. Please mail to:

Dr. Joan M. George
67 Stevens Ave.
Old Bridge, NJ 08857

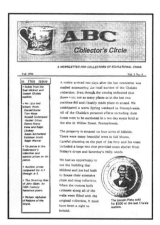

Dr. Joan M. George, publisher of *ABC Collector's Circle*.

~ INTRODUCTION ~

Few areas of collecting offer the variety or the charm of children's dishes. Manufactured of many materials for almost two centuries, on both sides of the Atlantic, plates, mugs, cups, and other utensils are still readily available to the collector.

Children's utensils were manufactured with and without letters of the alphabet. This book will concentrate on lettered material only, and will categorize and illustrate the Irene Lindsay collection.

Most of the book will feature English Staffordshire (soft paste) ABC plates and mugs. These plates were a challenge to categorize. We made the attempt in an effort to assist the beginning or advanced collector to keep track of their purchases. There are about 700 different English plates extant. Please understand, too, that a serious and continuing effort must be made at collecting ABC plates before one acquires those which fall into categories. Most collectors will find that they will prefer one category over another, birds over sports, for instance, and they will naturally concentrate on their interest. They will, in time, acquire variations of a design, and may decide to trade these with other collectors. Exact duplicates are rare.

A word about deep dish bowls. Irene has a few ABC bowls, usually those which are part of a set, but she prefers flat plates because they are easier to display.

After English soft paste, this book features German hard paste ABC ware, which is an attractive category to collect in itself. Manufacture began circa 1880, much later than England.

Tin, American and English, follows, then Litho tin, under its own heading.

American china is next. Although lacking the variety of English ABC material, we felt our native product was different enough to merit its own category.

Glass plates comprise the last category of ABC material.

~ CATEGORIES ~

Every item pictured in this book will have an identification number along with the item's size (diameter for plates, height for mugs and cups, length for others) and manufacturer's marks. For instance, EP-AW1 means "English plate — Animals, Wild 1 (the first plate in the series).

Categories begin with plates, the most numerous product, then mugs (cups, if tin), sets, and miscellaneous.

ABC mugs and cups are getting very hard to find and are quite expensive. Sets are even rarer. Each of these sub-categories will have an inclusive value for it in the paragraph at its beginning. It is difficult to assign a fair value to some sets, for instance, which are seldom seen. We advise a collector not to pass up a rare item if it is in good condition but priced more than the book value. We also urge him or her not to go through an antique show, planning to return to a booth where a plate or two is priced right — they won't be there when you return. If it's OK, buy it now.

In the ABC collecting field, sets are rare. Most examples seen are "almost" sets, cup, saucer, and plate in "almost" the same color, or with "almost" the same illustration. In our opinion, the various parts of a set are worth less if not a set — that is, a cup's value is $75.00 by itself, but more than that if it is with its original saucer and plate.

As one's collection grows, we suggest purchasing 3" x 5" file cards, along with a covered box, and making out a card, with photo, for each new treasure. The dividers which come with the cards can be used to separate the cards into categories. If taking photos is not convenient, you can copy the plate right out of this book and paste the copy on the back of the card.

After a couple of years of collecting, most people need to take their records with them to shows, to make sure they don't purchase duplicates. Variations of certain transfer designs occur, and the individual collector must decide if a variation is different enough to warrant its purchase.

⚐ *BRITISH REGISTRY TABLES* ⚐

This diamond-shaped registry mark stamped on some plates and mugs indicates the day, month, and year the design was registered. The mark also includes the material of manufacture and the company, from 1842 to 1883. According to an authority on British pottery, the actual date of manufacture was within three years of the design registration date.

ENGLISH REGISTRY MARKS 1842 - 1867

A. Material type: I-metal, II-wood, III-glass, IV-ceramics
B. Year registered
C. Month   "
D. Day   "
E. "Parcel" number- code indicating company

LETTERS INDICATING YEARS 1842-1867				LETTERS INDICATING MONTHS	
X-1842	S-1849	D-1856	R-1863	C-January	I-July
H-1843	V-1850	K-1857	N-1864	G-February	R-August
C-1844	P-1851	B-1858	W-1865	W-March	D-September
A-1845	D-1852	M-1859	Q-1866	H-April	B-October
I-1846	Y-1853	Z-1860	T-1867	E-May	K-November
F-1847	J-1854	R-1861		M-June	A-December
U-1848	E-1855	O-1862			

ENGLISH REGISTRY MARKS 1868 - 1883

A. Material type: I-metal, II-wood, III-glass, IV-ceramics
B. Day registered
C. "Parcel" number- code indicating company
D. Year registered
E. Month   "

LETTERS INDICATING YEARS 1868-1883			LETTERS INDICATING MONTHS	
X-1868	U-1874	J-1880	C-January	I-July
H-1869	S-1875	E-1881	G-February	R-August
C-1870	V-1876	L-1882	W-March	D-September
A-1871	P-1877	K-1883	H-April	B-October
I-1872	D-1878		E-May	K-November
F-1873	Y-1879		M-June	A-December

After 1883, the diamond registry marks were discontinued and a new system, consisiting of Rd No followed by a number, was used. The table below lists the numbers followed by the years registered. For instance, Staffordshire plates EP-B2, B4, B13, and B16, all stamped Rd No 154, were registered in 1884. Interestingly, on many Rd No marked plates, the manufacturer's name does not appear.

Registration Numbers, 1884-1991

1 = 1884	574817 = 1911	825231 = 1938	919607 = 1965
19754 = 1885	594195 = 1912	832610 = 1939	924510 = 1966
40480 = 1886	612431 = 1913	837520 = 1940	929335 = 1967
64520 = 1887	630190 = 1914	838590 = 1941	934515 = 1968
90483 = 1888	644935 = 1915	839230 = 1942	939875 = 1969
116648 = 1889	653521 = 1916	839980 = 1943	944932 = 1970
141273 = 1890	658988 = 1917	841040 = 1944	950046 = 1971
163767 = 1891	662872 = 1918	842670 = 1945	955342 = 1972
185713 = 1892	666128 = 1919	845550 = 1946	960708 = 1973
205240 = 1893	673750 = 1920	849730 = 1947	965185 = 1974
224720 = 1894	680147 = 1921	853260 = 1948	969249 = 1975
246975 = 1895	687144 = 1922	856999 = 1949	973838 = 1976
268392 = 1896	694999 = 1923	860854 = 1950	978426 = 1977
291241 = 1897	702671 = 1924	863970 = 1951	982815 = 1978
311658 = 1898	710165 = 1925	866280 = 1952	987910 = 1979
331707 = 1899	718057 = 1926	869300 = 1953	993012 = 1980
351202 = 1900	726330 = 1927	872531 = 1954	998302 = 1981
368154 = 1901	734370 = 1928	876067 = 1955	1004456 = 1982
385180 = 1902	742725 = 1929	879282 = 1956	1010583 = 1983
403200 = 1903	751160 = 1930	882949 = 1957	1017131 = 1984
424400 = 1904	760583 = 1931	887079 = 1958	1024174 = 1985
447800 = 1905	769670 = 1932	891665 = 1959	1031358 = 1986
471860 = 1906	779292 = 1933	895000 = 1960	1039055 = 1987
493900 = 1907	789019 = 1934	899914 = 1961	1047799 = 1988
518640 = 1908	799097 = 1935	904638 = 1962	1056078 = 1989
535170 = 1909	808794 = 1936	909364 = 1963	2003720 = 1990
552000 = 1910	817293 = 1937	914536 = 1964	2012047 = 1991

FROM GODDEN'S GUIDE TO ENGLISH PORCELAIN BY GEOFFREY GODDEN (WALLACE-HOMESTEAD BOOKS, $39.95).

⚓ VALUES ⚓

Many factors are involved in determining the value of anything, especially antiques. Age, rarity, and condition all come into play. Some categories of ABC material are quite scarce and therefore expensive. Each category in this book will feature an informational paragraph at its beginning, with a value range — $100.00 – 150.00, for instance. This is the amount the item is worth to most collectors. In a few categories, values vary between pieces, so each piece will have its value in the caption.

These values assume the piece is in good condition. Value parallels condition. Any cracks or chips detract from a piece's appearance and value. A glazed-over chip means the fault occurred during the manufacture of the piece and has little effect on its value. Even so, it's better if the chip is on the underside. Hairlines and spiders are sometimes seen and detract from a piece's value. Damaged or repaired ABC material sells for a fraction of the price of perfect pieces.

Crazing, tiny cracks under the glaze, and staining do not affect value. Crazing does not indicate china's age, and staining may be bleached out, although we prefer to let pieces so affected alone.

Of course, an experienced collector will come upon an unusual or seldom seen plate and know instinctively to snap it up, even if it means paying more than the book value. If you pass up a rare plate or mug to save $30.00 or $50.00 you may never get another chance at it.

Values listed in this book are the result of constant trips to antique shows, shops, flea markets, etc. in Pennsylvania and neighboring states.

The supply of ABC plates and mugs is supposedly stable, but is in reality diminishing, as material disappears into collections, is destroyed in fires, etc. Increasing collector interest with a diminishing supply means rising prices.

People collect for different reasons, but it would be difficult to find a more enjoyable collecting hobby or a better investment than ABC plates.

⚓ ENGLISH STAFFORDSHIRE PLATES ⚓

The following English ABC plate category is by far the largest of the book. Every effort was made to properly identify and illustrate each piece as well as to group it with others of the same subject. Most collectors concentrate on a favorite area, and it is our hope that this section will show most of what is available.

English plates, being made much earlier than German or American, tend to be more crude in their manufacture and less sophisticated in their subject matter. All illustrations were added by the transfer process. The alphabet can be transfer also or embossed into the china itself around the rim.

Some plates feature a transfer of one color, after which the plate was fired. The polychrome plates were hand colored after the initial transfer was applied. The plates were then given a final firing, after which they were set out on wire racks to cool and harden. All old English plates have three indentations top and bottom caused by the racks on the not-quite-hardened plates.

Some English plates, usually the more colorful ones, have marks on the back, identifying the manufacturer and sometimes, when the plate design was registered. Plates manufactured from 1842 to 1883 used the diamond mark of the British Registry.

These registry tables are on page 6; using them will tell the collector when his or her plate design was registered. Some marks were transferred, others were stamped or pressed onto the soft paste. Sometimes these marks are hard to read, but when one has a number of plates to examine, usually the maker can be identified. Also, pieces by the same manufacturer tend to have a similar appearance.

The English plate category is the most numerous, colorful, and say many collectors, the most interesting of all ABC categories.

AESOP'S FABLES

Apparently only a few of the more than 200 Aesop's Fables were chosen as subjects for ABC plates. The first four plates in this category are unmarked as to maker and fable, but the two scenes illustrate the fable "The man, the boy, and the donkey." The balance of the plates are transfers and plates six through eleven, although unmarked as to maker, are believed to have been made by Brownhills Pottery, Tunstall, circa 1875.

Monochrome $120.00 – 135.00

Polychrome $150.00 – 230.00

EP-AF1. 8¹/₂". No mark. Man and boy carrying donkey.

EP-AF2. 7". No mark. Man and boy carrying donkey.

EP-AF3. 7". No mark. Man and boy riding donkey.

EP-AF4. 7".   No mark. Man and boy riding donkey.

EP-AF5. 6¹/₂".   Pountney and Allies, 1816 – 1835. *The crow and the pitcher.*

EP-AF6. 7". No mark. *The lion and the mouse.*

EP-AF7. 6¹/₂". No mark. *The hare and the tortoise.*

EP-AF8. 5¹/₂". No mark. *The cock and the fox.*

EP-AF9. 7¹/₂". No mark. *The wolf and the crane.*

EP-AF10. 8". No mark. *The dog in the manger.*

EP-AF11. 8". No mark. *The fox and the grapes.*

This category covers household pets, cats, and dogs, plus what may be called barnyard animals. When these plates were made, most rural English families owned a cow for milk, a horse for farming, fowl for eggs and meat, and perhaps a pony for the children.

These plates were made by a number of potteries, with both transfer and embossed alphabets, and must have had great appeal for children.

Monochrome $110.00 – 125.00

Polychrome $145.00 – 180.00

EP-AD1. 7¹/₄". W Adams & Co., Tunstall, England (1891). Horse.

EP-AD2. 7¹/₄". Same as EP-AD1 but different color.

EP-AD3. 8¼". J. Meir & Son, Tunstall, England. Horse with birds.

EP-AD4. 8¼". W. Adams & Co., Tunstall, England. Dog with reading glasses.

EP-AD5. 7". No mark. Cat playing with mouse.

EP-AD6. 7¼". W Adams & Co., England. Cat.

EP-AD7. 7". Adams circular trademark.
In a soft place.

EP-AD8. 6³/₄". No mark. Cows, sheep in a pond.

EP-AD9. 7¹/₄". No mark. *The dog.*

EP-AD10. 7¹/₂". C.A. & Son, England (Charles Allerton). ***My face is my fortune.***

EP-AD11. 7". No mark. *Blood relations.*

EP-AD12. 7¹/₄" deep dish. No mark. Donkey in barn.

EP-AD13. 6¹/₂". No mark. *The donkey.*

EP-AD14. 6". No mark. Chickens.

EP-AD15. 6". No mark. Three goats.

EP-AD16. 5". No mark. *Cat and kittens.*

≈ *ANIMALS, WILD* ≈

Among the most beautiful of all of the English plates, the Wild Animal series was produced by a number of potteries. The transfer letter plates were made by the Brownhills Pottery, Tunstall, 1872 – 1896, and are marked with the British registry diamond, which dates the design.

Monochrome $125.00 – 150.00

Polychrome $150.00 – 225.00

EP-AW1. 7¹/₂". B.P. Co. *Bear with cubs.*

EP-AW2. 8¹/₂". B.P. Co. *Camel.*

EP-AW3. 7¹/₄". B.P. Co. *Elephant.*

EP-AW4. 7¹/₄". B.P. Co. *Leopard.*

EP-AW5. 7¹/₂". B.P. Co. *Lion.*

EP-AW6. 8¹/₄". B.P. Co. *Stag*.

EP-AW7. 6¹/₂". B.P. Co. *Tiger*.

EP-AW8. 7". Wm Adams & Co., Tunstall. Ferret.

EP-AW9. 7". Wm Adams & Co., Tunstall. Weasel.

EP-AW10. 7". No mark. *A sly fox.*

EP-AW11. 6". J. Meir & Son, Tunstall. Fox (?).

EP-AW12. 6". Powell & Bishop, 1876 – 1878. Zebra.

EP-AW13. 7". C.A. & Sons (Charles Allerton), 1890 – 1912. *A fishing elephant.*

EP-AW14. 6". No mark. Squirrel.

EP-AW15. 8". No mark. *Stag and fawn.*

EP-AW16. 6½". C.A. & Sons. *A timely rescue.*

EP-AW17. 7". No mark. *Fox and goose.*

One of the problems with separating a large number of plates into categories is the profusion of material illustrating one subject. We have included adults only in this category, adults with children under FAMILY LIFE, and adults working under OCCUPATIONS.

Monochrome $110.00 – 125.00

Polychrome $135.00 – 145.00

EP-AS1. 6". No mark. Man with Alpine horn and dog.

EP-AS2. 6". No mark. Same as EP-AS1 but polychrome.

EP-AS3. 5¹/₂". No mark. *Highland dance.*

EP-AS4. 7". No mark. Adults dancing.

EP-AS5. 7¹/₂". No mark. Adults in country scene.

EP-AS6. 5³/₄". No mark. Lovers.

EP-AS7. 7". No mark. *The walk.*

EP-AS8. 6". No mark. *The drive.*

EP-AS9. 7". Edge Malkin & Co. Women on bridge.

EP-AS10. 5". Edge Malkin & Co. Man seated with basket.

This is a very colorful category and certainly a favorite among our collector friends. BIRDS also features many different alphabet arrangements — the designers at the potteries really came up with some innovative and attractive patterns. Edge Malkin & Co. Pottery made some of these but sometimes its product is marked with an incuse stamp which can be hard to read. Edge Malkin also used a transfer "E.M. & Co." inside a decorative oval.

Monochrome $100.00 – 130.00

Polychrome $130.00 – 150.00

EP-B1. 7¹/₄". No mark. Crane and toad.

EP-B2. 6¹/₂". Rd No 154 (Brownhills Pottery). Dove.

EP-B3. 6³/₄". No mark. *Canary, bullfinch, and goldfinch.*

EP-B4. 7¹/₄". Rd No 154. *Goldfinch.*

EP-B5. 7". No mark. *The Kestrel.*

EP-B6. 6¹/₄". Edge Malkin & Co. *Kingfisher.*

EP-B7. 7¹/₄". Edge Malkin & Co. *Magpie.*

EP-B8. 7". No mark. *The Martin.*

EP-B9. 6¹/₄". Edge Malkin & Co. *Nightingale.*

EP-B10. 6". Edge Malkin & Co. *Birds of Paradise.*

EP-B11. 7¼". No mark. *Peacock*.

EP-B12. 6". Edge Malkin & Co. *House Sparrow*.

EP-B13. 8". Rd No 154. *Swallow*.

EP-B14. 5". No mark. *The young swans*.

EP-B15. 7". Rd No 154. *Titmouse.*

EP-B16. 8". Rd No 154. *Wandering Pie.*

EP-B17. 7¹/₄". No mark. Owls and bunny.

EP-B18. 7¹/₂". A. Shaw & Son. Bird and flowers.

EP-B19. 7¹/₂". A. Shaw & Son. Bird and morning glorys.

EP-B20. 7". No mark. *The golden crested wren.*

EP-B21. 6". Edge Malkin & Co. *Sky Lark.*

Since ABC plates and mugs were made for use by children, it stands to reason that many of the illustrations featured children. In fact, fully 20 percent of the English plates in this book use children in the transfer center.

To divide over 100 plates into manageable categories, we elected to begin with CHILDREN (alone or with other children), then CHILDREN'S RHYMES AND STORIES, CHILDREN WITH PETS, CHILDREN AT PLAY, and finally, CHILDREN AT WORK OR STUDY.

We made five "children" categories so a collector using this book for reference will locate a particular plate more easily when he or she sees one for sale.

Monochrome $110.00 – 130.00

Polychrome $130.00 – 145.00

EP-C1. 6¹/₄". Edge Malkin & Co. Children under umbrella.

EP-C2. 7". No mark. Two girls and flowers.

EP-C3. 7¹/₄". Mfg. for H.C. Edmiston, England. *At the seaside.*

EP-C4. 8". No mark. *The Garden Flower.*

EP-C5. 5". No mark. *The Graces.*

EP-C6. 7". Staffordshire, England. Girls with umbrellas.

EP-C7. 7". Powell & Bishop. *Baby*.

EP-C8. 7¹/₂". H.A. & Co. (H. Aynsley & Co., Longton). Girl in flowers.

EP-C9. 7¹/₂". No mark. Boy with stringed instrument eating bread at fence.

EP-C10. 6³/₄". No mark. Same as EP-C9 but smaller and different color.

EP-C11. 8¹/₄". No mark. *Lost.*

EP-C12. 6¹/₄". No mark. Same as EP-C11 but different size.

EP-C13. 6¹/₂". No mark. *The cruel boy.*

We have included nursery rhymes in this category. Brownhills Pottery (B.P.) is well represented here with its British Registry numbers. Almost all of the plates are transfer alphabet. Also included here are some modern English plates with mechanically applied illustrations. These are listed as "not old," with values.

Monochrome $120.00 – 135.00

Polychrome $150.00 – 230.00

EP-CRS1. 8½". No mark. *Nursery Rhymes — Goosey Goosey Gander.*

EP-CRS2. 8". Rd No 75,500, England (Brownhills Pottery). *Nursery Tales — Whittington and His Cat.*

EP-CRS3. 7". Rd No 149644 (B.P.). *Red Riding Hood and her supposed grandmother.*

EP-CRS4. 7¼". Rd No 149644. *Red Riding Hood starting.* Note: This plate has a sticker in the back stating Nathan's — always the cheapest — Johnstown Pa — 10¢.

EP-CRS5. 7¼". Rd No 75,500. *Nursery Tales — Little Jack Horner.*

EP-CRS6. 7¼". Rd No 75,500. *Nursery Tales — Cinderella.*

EP-CRS7. 7¹/₄". Rd No 75,500. *Nursery Tales — Old Mother Hubbard.*

EP-CRS8. 8¹/₄". No mark. *Nursery Rhymes — Ding Dong Bell.*

EP-CRS9. 7¹/₂". No mark. *Nursery Rhymes — There was a crooked man.*

EP-CRS10. 6¹/₂". No mark. *There was a crooked man.*

EP-CRS11. 6¹/₂". No mark. *Simple Simon.*

EP-CRS12. 5¹/₂". No mark. *Old Mother Hubbard.*

EP-CRS13. 7". 3H2Z incuse mark. *See saw Margery Daw....*

EP-CRS14. 6". Manufactured for H.C. Edmiston, England. *Little Boo Peep.*

EP-CRS15. 5". Same as EP-CRS14 but a saucer.

EP-CRS16. 6". J. & G. Meakin (1851 – 1890). *The tulip and the butterfly....*

EP-CRS17. 7". Lord Nelson Pottery, plate is dated 11/76. Simple Simon. Not old. $30.00 – 40.00.

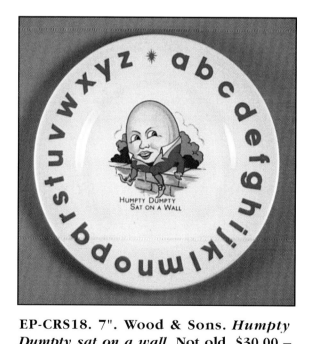

EP-CRS18. 7". Wood & Sons. *Humpty Dumpty sat on a wall.* **Not old. $30.00 – 40.00.**

EP-CRS19. 6¹/₂" deep dish. Wood & Sons. *Old Mother Hubbard*. Not old. $30.00 – 40.00.

EP-CRS20. 6¹/₂" deep dish. Wood & Sons. *Ride a cock horse....* Not old. $30.00 – 40.00.

EP-CRS21. 6³/₄". J.H. P & R, B & Ny. *Cinderella and the glass slipper.*

EP-CRS22. 6³/₄". J.H. P & R, B & Ny. *Little Jack Horner....*

EP-CRS23. 7". Incuse mark. *See saw Margery Daw....* Similar to EP-CRS13 except illustration is slightly different as is color.

EP-CRS24. 6½" deep dish. Wood and Sons, England. *Tom, Tom, the pipers son.* Not old. $30.00 – 40.00.

EP-CRS25. 7¼". *Paul and Virginia.*

This is a very colorful and charming category. The subjects illustrated must have been a great favorite of the children. Cats and dogs are shown, plus ponies, donkeys, rabbits, etc. Many of these pets are shown under ANIMALS, DOMESTIC but in this section, children are with their pets.

Monochrome $90.00 – 110.00

Polychrome $125.00 – 145.00

EP-CP1. 8". No mark. *Harry and his dog.*

EP-CP2. 8". "STONE WARE" impressed. *The sentinel.*

EP-CP3. 7¼". B.P. & Co. Children's clock. *Rupert and Spot.*

EP-CP4. 7½". No mark. Children with rabbit.

EP-CP5. 7". Powell & Bishop. *Feeding the donkey.*

EP-CP6. 6½". No mark. *Feeding my rabbits.*

EP-CP7. 7". Elsmore & Foster. *The guardian.*

EP-CP8. 6³/₄". No mark. *The new pony.*

EP-CP9. 8". No mark. Same as EP-CP8 except for color and size.

EP-CP10. 5". No mark. *The ride by the sea side.*

EP-CP11. 6". No mark. Same as EP-CP10 except for color and size.

EP-CP12. 5¹/₄". No mark. Child and horse.

EP CP13. 7". Elsmore & Son, England. Girls and ducks.

EP-CP14. 6". Elsmore & Foster. *The children trying....*

EP-CP15. 6¹/₄". No mark. Same as EP-CP14 except for coloring and size.

EP-CP16. 6". Elsmore & Foster. *Pretty Polly....*

EP-CP17. 6". J. Clementson, Shelton. *Oh look, brother....*

EP-CP18. 6". Elsmore & Foster. *That girl wants....*

EP-CP19. 6". No mark. *Our donkey and foal.*

EP-CP20. 7¹/₄". No mark. *The boy and his pony.*

EP-CP21. 7¹/₄". No mark. *The pride of the barnyard.*

EP-CP22. 7¹/₄". No mark. Two girls and a pony.

EP-CP23. 5". No mark. Girl, pony, dog, and chickens.

EP-CP24. 6". Edge, Malkin & Co. Same as EP-CP23 but larger.

EP-CP25. 6". No mark. *Willie and his rabbit.*

EP-CP26. 5¹/₂". Elsmore & Foster. *Catch it, Carlo....*

This category is the largest of the book; certainly it is no surprise that games and play were popular with children of all ages. The portrayals of children enjoying themselves with their innocent pastimes appeals to us today, and a collector could amass a very attractive group of plates on this subject alone.

The importance of the home and domestic affairs is continued in the category FAMILY LIFE, which has almost as many examples as CHILDREN AT PLAY.

Monochrome $120.00 – 135.00
Polychrome $135.00 – 145.00

EP-CPL1. 5½". No mark. *The young charioteer.*

EP-CPL2. 6". No mark. Child on chair with puppet.

EP-CPL3. 5³/₄". J.F. Wileman. *L' Hama Hammock.*

EP-CPL4. 6". No mark. **Boys playing leap frog.**

EP-CPL5. 6". No mark. *The playground.*

EP-CPL6. 6". No mark. *Little boys at marbles play.*

EP-CPL7. 5¹/₂". No mark. Boys playing marbles.

EP-CPL8. 5³/₄". No mark. Children on swing.

EP-CPL9. 5¹/₂". No mark. Children skating.

EP-CPL10. 6". No mark. *Playing at lovers.*

EP-CPL11. 6". J. & G. Meakin. *Peg-top.*

EP-CPL12. 6". Elsmore & Son, England. *Ready for a ride*.

EP-CPL13. 7". J & G. Meakin. *Stilt-walking*.

EP-CPL14. 7¹/₄". No mark. Child and bears on parade, two alphabets.

EP-CPL15. 7". No mark. Child and bears in canoe, two alphabets.

EP-CPL16. 7". Rd No 253083 (B.P. Co.). Children's clock. *A wheelbarrow ride.*

EP-CPL17. 5¹/₄". J. & G. Meakin. *Cricket.*

EP-CPL18. 5¹/₄". J. & G. Meakin. *Archery.*

EP-CPL19. 6¹/₄". No mark. *The first nibble.*

EP-CPL20. 6". J. & G. Meakin. *Kite-flying.*

EP-CPL21. 6". No mark. *Ship-building.*

EP-CPL22. 6". No mark. *Jump little nagtail.*

EP-CPL23. 7". No mark. Children on swing.

EP-CPL24. 7¹/₂". No mark. Children under umbrella with doll.

EP-CPL25. 8". No mark. *Swing swong*.

EP-CPL26. 6". No mark. Children with kite.

EP-CPL27. 8". No mark. *Oh here is old Robert....*

EP-CPL28. 7". Elsmore & Foster, Tunstall. *The young sergeant.*

EP-CPL29. 7¹/₄". No mark. *Thump away Jack....*

EP-CPL30. 5". No mark. Children at water with sailboat.

EP-CPL31. 6¹/₄". No mark. **Children playing at horses.**

EP-CPL32. 6¹/₄". No mark. **Dog, girl, bird, and flowers.**

EP-CPL33. 6". No mark. *Tom and Harry playing at horses.*

EP-CPL34. 6¹/₄". No mark. *Spinning tops.*

EP-CPL35. 6". J.F. Wileman. *Les Rondes — Romps.*

EP-CPL36. 7". No mark. *Frolics of youth — don't I look like Papa.*

EP-CPL37. 7¹/₄". J. & G. Meakin. *Top-whipping.*

EP-CPL38. 7". No mark. *The sick doll.*

EP-CPL39. 6¹/₂". No mark. **Children in yard.**

EP-CPL40. 6¹/₂". No mark. *Young artist.*

EP-CPL41. 8". No mark. **Two girls at piano.**

EP-CPL42. 7¹/₂". No. 940, Rd No, 153253, C. Allerton. **Girls with rake and watering can.**

EP-CPL43. 6³/₄". No. 940, Rd No 153253, Stafford-shire, England. Girls at bench stacking tops.

EP-CPL44. 8¹/₄". No mark. Children with scale and net.

EP-CPL45. 8¹/₄". No mark. Same as EP-CPL44 except for color.

EP-CPL46. 6¼". Powell & Bishop. Children playing ball.

EP-CPL47. 6¼". Powell & Bishop. Same as EP-CPL46 except for color.

EP-CPL48. 6". Powell & Bishop. Children playing and falling down.

EP-CPL49. 5". No mark. *Tired of play.*

EP-CPL50. 6". No mark. Same as EP-CPL49 except for size and color.

EP-CPL51. 7¹/₂". No mark. Double alphabet, girls on wall blowing soap bubbles.

This category was definitely not a popular one with the potters or children, since there are so few examples. Indeed, many of the plates in this book were manufactured using children as young as six years old in all phases of production. What seems unthinkable today took place as late as the middle of the nineteenth century. The large number of English ABC wares which survive today is due to their low price, which was made possible by using cheap child labor.

Monochrome $95.00 – 120.00

Polychrome $120.00 – 140.00

EP-CWS1. 5³/₄". No mark. *Spelling bee.*

EP-CWS2. 4³/₄". J.F. Wileman. Children reading a book.

EP-CWS3. 4³/₄". No mark. One child reading a book.

EP-CWS4. 7". No mark. Girl at piano. *The pretty child....*

EP-CWS5. 7". Elsmore & Son. Same as EP-CWS4 except for tinting.

EP-CWS6. 6". Edge Malkin & Co. Boy selling newspapers.

EP-CWS7. 8¹/₄". Edge Malkin & Co. Same as EP-CWS6 except for size and color.

These plates are cartoon strips on china. The large illustration in the center is the first panel; the four in the corners complete the strip. All of the plates tell a humorous story and they may use more than one plate to tell it. We considered putting Diamond plates under FUN, but felt the design of these plates is distinctive enough to merit its own category. Although only one plate has a manufacturer's mark, it is our opinion that the series was made by C.A. & Sons, England (Charles Allerton, Longton, 1859 – 1942).

Monochrome $110.00 – 135.00

Polychrome $135.00 – 150.00

EP-D1. 7¹/₂". C.A. & Sons, England. Rider rents horse.

EP-D2. 7¹/₂". No mark. Same plate as EP-D1 but polychrome.

EP-D3. 7¹/₂". No mark. Rider mounts horse, gets thrown.

EP-D4. 6³/₄". Staffordshire, England. Horse has just thrown rider.

EP-D5. 7¹/₂". Staffordshire, England. Rider mounts, is thrown, walks home.

EP-D6. 8³/₈". Staffordshire, England. Fisherman loses hat to wind, he retrieves it.

EP-D7. 7¹/₂". No mark. Fisherman naps while geese eat his lunch.

EP-D8. 8³/₈". Staffordshire, England. Artist sets up easel, children annoy him, they get spanked.

EP-D9. 8³/₈". Staffordshire, England. Animals annoy artist, he complains to farmer, man crowns artist with his own canvas.

This is the second largest category in the book. It contains ABC plates which depict all phases of home and family. Included are plates which could have been placed under other headings, but they are here because these particular plates illustrate the entire family involved in an activity, farming, for instance. We will be second guessed on some of these but we spent an inordinate amount of time on this category and think that the designers of these plates intended them to show FAMILY LIFE of nineteenth century England.

Monochrome $110.00 – 125.00

Polychrome $125.00 – 140.00

EP-FL1. 4¹/₂". J.&G. Meakin. Man plowing with horses.

EP-FL2. 5". No mark. Family gathering firewood.

EP-FL3. 5". No mark. Family harvesting wheat.

EP-FL4. 5". No mark. Family on picnic.

EP-FL5. 5". No mark. Family in canoe.

EP-FL6. 5¹/₂". No mark. Family in woods with basket.

EP-FL7. 5¼". Powell & Bishop. Mother and daughter in garden.

EP-FL8. 7¾". No mark. Family raking.

EP-FL9. 8". No mark. *Frolics of Youth — the young artist.* Older siblings.

EP-FL10. 7". Elsmore & Foster. *Mother and daughter dear to each.....*

EP-FL11. 8". No mark. Woman feeding chicken.

EP-FL12. 5". No mark. Man with horses resting from plowing.

EP-FL13. 4¹/₂". J. & G. Meakin. Family farming.

EP-FL14. 4¹/₂". J. & G. Meakin. Family with oxen gathering wheat.

EP-FL15. 4¹/₂". J. & G. Meakin. **Family and cows.**

EP-FL16. 5¹/₄". No mark. *The blind girl.*

EP-FL17. 7". No mark. *The field of wheat.*

EP-FL18. 5". No mark. **Woman feeding cows.**

EP-FL19. 6". No mark. Same as EP-FL18 except for size.

EP-FL20. 5". No mark. Mother with children and chicken.

EP-FL21. 6". No mark. Same as EP-FL20 except for size.

EP-FL22. 6". Edge Malkin & Co. Family in canoe.

EP-FL23. 6". Edge Malkin & Co. Same as EP-FL22 except for color.

EP-FL24. 6¹/₂". No mark. Family on picnic.

EP-FL25. 6³/₄". No mark. Same as EP-FL24 except for size and color.

EP-FL26. 7¹/₂". C.A. & Sons, England. Family on picnic with horse at water.

EP-FL27. 4¹/₄". **J. & G. Meakin. Woman at mirror with family.**

EP-FL28. 4¹/₂". **J. & G. Meakin. Same as EP-FL27 except for size and color.**

EP-FL29. 5¹/₂". **No mark.** *How doth the little busy bee....*

EP-FL30. 7¹/₄". **No mark. Same as EP-FL29 except for size and color.**

EP-FL31. 4³/₄". J.F. Wileman. Woman working in kitchen.

EP-FL32. 4³/₄". J.F. Wileman. Mother reading to children.

EP-FL33. 5". No mark. Ladies having tea.

EP-FL34. 4¹/₂". No mark. Elderly man and woman with dog.

EP-FL35. 6". No mark. **Woman with basket with little girl.**

EP-FL36. 5¹/₂". No mark. **Elderly man with child in garden.**

EP-FL37. 6". No mark. *The barn.*

EP-FL38. 6¹/₄". No mark. *The pet.*

EP-FL39. 6¹/₄". No mark. *The seed in the ground.*

EP-FL40. 6". J. & G. Meakin. *Harvest-home.*

This category illustrates the personal traits which were deemed desireable for children to acquire. Each plate illustrated a virtue, which was followed by a poem that encircled the transfer illustration. All of the alphabets are embossed.

Monochrome $120.00 – 135.00

Polychrome $135.00 – 155.00

EP-FNF1. 5³/₄". J. & G. Meakin (incuse: hard to read). *Cheerfulness.*

EP-FNF2. 7¹/₄". No mark. *Meekness.*

EP-FNF3. 7". No mark. *Attention.*

EP-FNF4. 7¹/₄". No mark. *Industry.*

EP-FNF5. 7". No mark. *Early Rising.*

EP-FNF6. 7". England. *Charity.*

EP-FNF7. 6". No mark. *Devotion.*

Another large, and very colorful, category with an American connection. These plates illustrate Poor Richard's, Dr. Franklin's, and Franklin's, maxims or proverbs, and have such a number of variations that it is beyond the scope of this book to spell everything out. We elected to list the plate title and the first few words of the maxim or proverb, the illustration of the plate in the book completing the reference.

Monochrome $125.00 – 140.00

Polychrome $140.00 – 165.00

EP-FP1. 5". No mark. *Experience keeps....*

EP-FP2. 6". No mark. Same as EP-FP1 except for size and color.

EP-FP3. 7". No mark. *Dost thou love life....*

EP-FP4. 8¹/₄". No mark. Same as EP-FP3 except for size and color.

EP-FP5. 6". No mark. *For age and want....*

EP-FP6. 8¹/₄". No mark. Same as EP-FP5 except for size and color.

EP-FP7. 5". No mark. *There are no gains....*

EP-FP8. 6". No mark. Same as EP-FP7 except for size and color.

EP-FP9. 7¹/₂". No mark. *Employ time well....*

EP-FP10. 7¹/₂". No mark. Same as EP-FP9 except for color.

EP-FP11. 8". No mark. *Plough deep while....*

EP-FP12. 6". No mark. *If you would know....*

EP-FP13. 6". No mark. *Little strokes fell....*

EP-FP14. 7¹/₄". No mark. *Constant dropping wears....*

EP-FP15. 7¹/₄". No mark. *Dr. Franklin's Maxims, Want of care....*

EP-FP16. 6¼". No mark. Same as EP-FP15 except for size and color.

EP-FP17. 7". No mark. *Dr. Franklin's Maxims, By diligence and....*

EP-FP18. 6¼". No mark. *Sloth like rust....*

EP-FP19. 6¼". No mark. *He that hath....*

EP-FP20. 6". No mark. Same as EP-FP19 except for size, color, and transfer.

EP-FP21. 8¹/₄". No mark. Same as EP-FP19 except for size and color.

EP-FP22. 5³/₄". J. & G. Meakin. *Franklin's Proverbs, Three removes....*

EP-FP23. 7¹/₄". No mark. Same as EP-FP22 except for size and scene.

EP-FP24. 8¹/₄". No mark. Same as EP-FP22 except for size and color.

EP-FP25. 7". J. & G. Meakin. *Keep thy shop....*

EP-FP26. 6". *Franklin's Proverbs, Silks and satins....*

EP-FP27. 7". J. & G. Meakin *Franklin's Proverbs, He that by the....*

EP-FP28. 7". J. & G. Meakin. *Franklin's Proverbs, Make hay while....*

EP-FP29. 8". J & G. Meakin. Same as EP-FP28 except for size.

EP-FP30. 5". No mark. *Poor Richard's Maxims, Fly pleasure and....*

EP-FP31. 7". No mark. *Poor Richard's Way to Wealth, Fly pleasures....*

EP-FP32. 6". No mark. _Not to oversee...._

EP-FP33. 7". No mark. _The eye of the...._

EP-FP34. 6". No mark. _Now I have a...._

EP-FP35. 6¹/₄". No mark. Same as EP-FP34 except for size and *Dr. Franklin* at bottom of plate.

EP-FP36. 7". J. & G. Meakin. Same as EP-FP34 except for size and *Franklin's Proverbs* at bottom of plate.

EP-FP37. 5³/₄". No mark. *Employ time well....*

EP-FP38. 7¹/₂". No mark. Same as EP-FP37 except for size and color.

EP-FP39. 5¹/₂". No mark. *There are no....*

EP-FP40. 8". Adams. *Importance of punctuality....*

We called this category FUN instead of HUMOR because HUMOR is too close to HUNTING for our identification system.

Many of the humorous scenes in this category are of the pratfall or slapstick type. The single illustrations had to deliver a punch line immediately, in contrast to the humor of the DIAMOND PLATES, which have five panels to do so. Some of these plates use animals acting like humans, which we also see today in comic strips.

Monochrome $130.00 – 140.00

Polychrome $140.00 – 165.00

EP-FUN1. 6¹/₄". No mark. *Who are you.*

EP-FUN2. 7¹/₂". No mark. *Itinerant musician.*

EP-FUN3. 5". No mark. *Off with him.*

EP-FUN4. 5". No mark. *Snuffing*.

EP-FUN5. 7¹/₄". No mark. Three cats pulling tablecloth.

EP-FUN6. 8". Elsmore & Son, England. Buck jumping hunter.

EP-FUN7. 8". Elsmore & Son, England. Three dogs walking tightrope.

EP-FUN8. 6¹/₂". Staffordshire, England. Boy on fence stealing apples.

EP-FUN9. 7¹/₄". Elsmore & Son, England. Dogs stealing food from table.

EP-FUN10. 7". No mark. *Donkey race — stop, Tom.*

EP-FUN11. 7¹/₄". No mark. *Mischief.*

EP-FUN12. 7³/₄". No mark. *An unwelcome guest.*

EP-FUN13. 7". Elsmore & Son, England. Two men riding bucking donkeys.

EP-FUN14. 8". No mark. Three kittens taking a bath.

EP-FUN15. 7¹/₂". No mark. Man in swamp, horses running.

EP-FUN16. 7". Elsmore & Son, England.
Man sleeping, children stealing hat.

EP-FUN17. 8". Allertons, England. *Come
into the garden Maude.*

EP-FUN18. 6¹⁄₂". Staffordshire, England.
Man falling down hill, deer watching.

EP-FUN19. 7¹⁄₄". C.A. & Sons, England.
Same as EP-FUN18 except for size and
color.

EP-FUN20. 6³/₄". **C.A. & Sons, England. Punch and Judy.**

EP-FUN21. 7¹/₂". **No mark. Same as EP-FUN20 except for size and color.**

EP-FUN22. 7¹/₄". **C.A. & Sons, England. Punch and Judy with dog.**

EP-FUN23. 8". **Allertons, England. Punch and Judy with baby and smoking frog.**

EP-FUN24. 6³/₄". Charles Allerton and Sons, England. Dog and cart crash.

EP-FUN25. 6¹/₂". No mark. Same as EP-FUN24 except for size and color.

EP-FUN26. 7¹/₂". No mark. Same as EP-FUN24 except for size and color.

EP-FUN27. 6³/₄". No mark. Dog pulling cart with two children.

EP-FUN28. 8¹/₄". No mark. Same as EP-FUN27 except for size and color.

EP-FUN29. 7¹/₂". Staffordshire, England. Bull charging man.

EP-FUN30. 6". No mark. Two men boxing. ***Practice.***

EP-FUN31. 8". No mark. ***A lecture on the cold water cure.***

EP-FUN32. 6¹/₂". No mark. ***Awkward squad.***

Shown are fox and deer hunting scenes from nineteenth century England; almost all involve dogs and horses.

Monochrome $90.00 – 125.00

Polychrome $130.00 – 150.00

EP-H1. 6". No mark. Stag and hounds.

EP-H2. 6¹/₂". C.A. & Sons, England. Two dogs and two men with rifles.

EP-H3. 7¹/₂". No mark. Same as EP-H2 except for size and color.

EP-H4. 5". J. & G. Meakin. Men on hunt.

EP-H5. 6". No mark. Same as EP-H4 except for size and color.

EP-H6. 6³/₄". No mark. Hunter and two dogs.

EP-H7. 5¹/₂". No mark. Horseman with spear and buffalo.

EP-H8. 5". No mark. Hunters on horses.

EP-H9. 6³/₄". Staffordshire, England. Two horses and dogs.

EP-H10. 7". No mark. Two horsemen, two dogs.

EP-H11. 7¹/₄". No mark. Two horsemen, dogs at gate.

EP-H12. 6³/₄". Staffordshire, England. Two dogs, men.

EP-H13. 7". No mark. *Wild horse hunt.*

EP-H14. 7¹/₄". No mark. Man shooting ducks with dogs.

EP-H15. 7¹/₄". No mark. Horseman, dogs, and men.

EP-H16. 7³/₄". No mark. Two dogs, hunter with dead fox.

As far as we know, these three are the only plates on this subject. Made by C.A. & Sons, England (Charles Allerton), in at least two single color transfers with embossed alphabet, these plates feature very well done illustrations.

Monochrome only $150.00 – 160.00

EP-IA1. 8". C.A. & Sons, England. *Chinonca watching the departure of the cavalcade.*

EP-IA2. 7". C.A. & Sons, England. *A Sioux Indian chief.*

EP-IA3. 6¹/₂". C.A. & Sons, England. *The candle fish.*

We have included both large capital letters plates — these have words beginning with those letters — and plates with a poem and illustration describing the letter. We are sure there must have been complete sets of 26 letters but have never seen such a set.

Monochrome $100.00 – 125.00

Polychrome $125.00 – 185.00

EP-LA1. 5³/₄". Charles Allerton & Sons, England. ABC.

EP-LA2. 6". No mark. *Apple, ape, air.*

EP-LA3. 5". No mark. *Boat, bat, ball.*

EP-LA4. 7". No mark. *B is for Bobby's....*

EP-LA5. 6¹⁄₂". No mark. *F is for the fowls....*

EP-LA6. 7". No mark. Same as EP-LA5 except for size and color.

EP-LA7. 6¹/₄". No mark. *Pig, pigeon, pins.*

EP-LA8. 7¹/₄". No mark. *P is for Peter....*

EP-LA9. 6¹/₄". No mark. *Vixen.*

EP-LA10. 5¹/₂". Staffordshire, England. *Y, Z.*

EP-LA11. 5³/₄". Staffordshire, England. *V, W, X.*

EP-LA12. 7¹/₄". No mark. *T* (pink transfer).

EP-LA13. 7". No mark. *T — T is for Timothy....*

Another category with an American flavor, many of the scenes and personalities are from our Civil War (1861 – 1865). Seeing the similarities of some plates, these must have been made in sets.

Monochrome $165.00 – 185.00

Polychrome $185.00 – 350.00

EP-ML1. 5". No mark. *Major General N.P. Banks.*

EP-ML2. 5". No mark. *Major General Geo. G. Meade.*

EP-ML3. 5". J.F. Wileman. Soldier tipping his chapeau.

EP-ML4. 6". No mark. *Arrival of General McClellan.*

EP-ML5. 6". No mark. *Union troops in Virginia.*

EP-ML6. 6³/4". C.A. & Sons, England. Two soldiers training.

EP-ML7. 7". No mark. *Federal Generals.*

EP-ML8. 6¹/₂". C.A. Sons, England. Soldier on horseback fighting foot soldier.

EP-ML9. 7¹/₄". No mark. Pipe-smoking soldier posing for his portrait.

EP-ML10. 7¹/₄". No mark. *Incidents of the war — a convalescent from Inkermann.*

Included here is every plate we couldn't honestly put in any other category. We tried very hard to identify each subject and place it in a category with others of its kind; this makes the book easier to use, but the plates here, for one reason or another, wouldn't fit anywhere else.

Monochromes $110.00 – 130.00

Polychromes $130.00 – 165.00

EP-MS1. 5". No mark. *Chinese amusement — my pretty pheasant.*

EP-MS2. 5¹/₄". No mark. Leaves with buds.

EP-MS3. 5". No mark. Leaves with flowers and buds.

EP-MS4. 7". No mark. Floral transfer.

EP-MS5. 7". No mark. Same as EP-MS4 except for color and transfer.

EP-MS6. 6³/₄". No mark. House with people and large tree.

EP-MS7. 5³/₄". No mark. *Contentment makes the believer rich.*

EP-MS8. 6¹/₄". No mark. House — pink luster.

EP-MS9. 6". Mackwood. *Ter Gedachtenis* (day of your birth).

EP-MS10. 6¹/₂". No mark. Squirrel in leaves.

EP-MS11. 7". Edge Malkin & Co. Train.

EP-MS12. 5³/₄". England. Castle with couple walking.

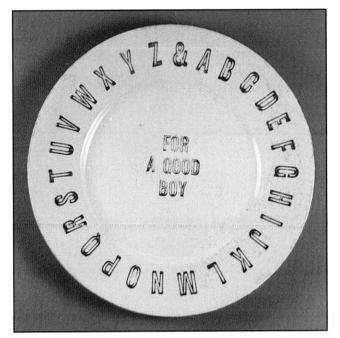

EP-MS13. 7¹/₄". Extra Quality Ironstone China, Warranted. *For a good boy.*

EP-MS14. 7¹/₄". No mark. *Crossing the plains.*

EP-MS15. 7¹/₂". Rd No 74762. Clock face.

EP-MS16. 8". No mark. *Have I found you at last?*

EP-MS17. 7". No mark. *Uncle Tom's Cabin — death of Uncle Tom.*

EP-MS18. 7". No mark. Double alphabet with bridge, windmill, and stream.

Assuming that complete sets of 12 were manufactured in this category, we can only wonder what happened to them. Months of the year plates are seldom seen and two from the same series may be considered a real prize.

Monochrome $110.00 – 120.00

Polychrome $120.00 – 150.00

EP-M1. 6³/₄". No mark. *April.*

EP-M2. 7¹/₂". No mark. *June.*

EP-M3. 7¹/₄". No mark. *August.*

EP-M4. 6¹/₂". No mark. *October.*

Not a large category, certainly, but an interesting one, the plates showing work day life of England during the nineteenth century.

Plate EP-02 illustrates something seen occasionally on transfer plates: part of the transfer didn't transfer and the grindstone on EP-O1 became a rocking chair on EP-O2. It was handpainted, as well as the blacksmith and part of the building. A couple of the plates in the FRANKLIN'S PROVERBS category have similar flaws, which really do not affect value.

Monochrome $100.00 – 130.00

Polychrome $130.00 – 150.00

EP-O1. 5¹/₄". No mark. *The village blacksmith.*

EP-O2. 6". No mark. Same as EP-O1 except for size, color, and transfer.

EP-O3. 7". Powell & Bishop. *London dog seller.*

EP-O4. 5". No mark. *Fruit seller.*

EP-O5. 5". No mark. *The beggar.*

EP-O6. 4¹/₄". J. & G. Meakin. Street scene, person at stall.

EP-O7. 5". J. & G. Meakin. Postman.

EP-O8. 7". No mark. People in hay field.

EP-O9. 7¼". No mark. Organ grinder.

EP-O10. 8¼". Edge Malkin & Co., England. Girls playing music and tambourine.

EP-O11. 6". No mark. *The gleaners.*

EP-O12. 8". Elsmore & Son, England. *Going to market.*

EP-O13. 6". No mark. *Gathering cotton.*

EP-O14. 5¹/₂". No mark. Same as EP-O13 except for size and color.

Another category with few examples. All are single color transfer illustrations with embossed alphabets.

Monochrome $175.00 – 500.00

EP-PA1. 6$\frac{1}{2}$". No mark. William Penn.

EP-PA2. 6$\frac{3}{4}$". No mark. George Washington.

EP-PA3. 6$\frac{3}{4}$". No mark. James Garfield.

EP-PA4. 7$\frac{1}{2}$". No mark. Abraham Lincoln.

A natural enough subject, considering the country where the plates were manufactured, but we wonder why there are so few examples. Perhaps the children found the subject not to their liking.

Monochrome $150.00 – 165.00

Polychrome $165.00 – 450.00

EP-PE1. 5³/₄". No mark. *The late Sir Robert Peel Bart.*

EP-PE2. 7¹/₂". No mark. *Queen Victoria.*

EP-PE3. 7¹/₄". No mark. *Diverting history of John Gilpin.*

Included in this category are famous English and American landmarks, plus foreign scenes. Here, too, are examples of the beautiful Brownhills Pottery series "Famous Places" and "Nations of the World."

Monochrome $115.00 – 135.00

Polychrome $135.00 – 155.00

EP-P1. 5". No mark. Young dancer with tambourine.

EP-P2. 7¹/₄". No mark. *Landing place of the Pilgrims.*

EP-P3. 7". No mark. *Evening bathing scene at Manhatton Beach.*

EP-P4. 6³/₄". **No mark.** *Marine railway station Manhatton Beach Hotel.*

EP-P5. 6³/₄". **Trademark registered in US Patents Office.** *Electrical building, World's Columbian Exposition.*

EP-P6. 7". **No mark. Two camels, people and city in background.**

EP-P7. 6¹/₄". **No mark.** *Machinery Hall, World's Fair, Chicago.*

EP-P8. 7¹/₄". Staffordshire, England. *Electrical Building, World's Fair, Chicago.*

EP-P9. 6³/₄". Charles Allerton & Sons, England. Trademark Registered in US Patents Office. *Administration Building, World's Columbian Exposition.*

EP-P10. 6³/₄". No mark. *Brighton Beach Bathing Pavilion.*

EP-P11. 7¹/₂". No mark. *Hotel Brighton & Concourse.*

EP-P12. 8¼". No mark. *Iron pier. Length 1000 feet. West Brighton Beach.*

EP-P13. 7¾". No mark. Chinese country scene.

EP-P14. 7½". No mark. Two chinese men with peacock.

EP-P15. 5½". No mark. *Oriental Hotel.*

EP-P16. 7¹/₂". No mark. Same as EP-P15 except for size and color.

EP-P17. 7¹/₂". No mark. *Capitol at Washington.*

EP-P18. 7¹/₄". B.P. Co. Registry mark. *Nations of the World — Greek.*

EP-P19. 7¹/₄". B.P. Co. Registry mark. *Nations of the World — Japanese.*

EP-P20. 7¹/₄". Rd No 26734 B.P. Co. *Famous places — New York City Hall and Mount Vernon.*

EP-P21. 8". Rd No 26734 B.P. Co. *Famous places — Parliament House of Ottawa and Post Office of Ottawa.*

EP-P22. 8". Rd No 26734 B.P. Co. *Famous places — Niagara Falls Suspension Bridge and the White House Washington.*

EP-P23. 7¹/₄". B.P. Co. Registry mark. *Nations of the World — Wallachian.*

Enough colorful plates exist in this category for the collector to accumulate a very attractive wall display. Taken, as a rule, from Bible verses and stories, most of these plates have at least a title, and in most cases an entire verse, to explain the transfer illustration. Some of the plates must have been part of a set, and a number of different sets must have been manufactured.

Monochrome $115.00 – 125.00

Polychrome $130.00 – 180.00

EP-RL1. 5¹/₄". J. & G. Meakin. *Behold him rising....*

EP-RL2. 7¹/₄". J. & G.Meakin. Same as EP-RL1 except for size and color.

EP-RL3. 4³/₄" saucer. H.C. Edmiston, England. *The finding of Moses.*

EP-RL4. 6". H.C. Edmiston, England. *Noah and the ark.*

EP-RL5. 6". No mark. Minister speaking to three idlers.

EP-RL6. 7¼". Rd No 106738. *The destruction of Pharaoh.*

EP-RL7. 6". H.C. Edmiston, England. *David and Goliath.*

EP-RL8. 6". **J. & G. Meakin.** *At twelve years old....*

EP-RL9. 7¼". **No mark.** *A firm faith is the....*

EP-RL10. 6". **No mark.** *The world is the....*

EP-RL11. 6". No mark. *Band of Hope. The Sabbath keepers.*

EP-RL12. 5¹/₄". No mark. *The commandments. Thou shalt not....*

EP-RL13. 5". J. & G. Meakin. *I Lay my body....*

EP-RL14. 5". J. & G. Meakin. *Hush my dear....*

EP-RL15. 6". No mark. *Sacred history of Joseph.... Reuben interceding....*

EP-RL16. 6". No mark. *Sacred history of Joseph.... Joseph sold....*

There are two types of riddle plates in this category: one has the riddle on the face of the plate and its answer on the back; the other has the riddle and answer on the face, below the illustration. The first few of these plates came as a set.

Monochrome $125.00 – 140.00

Polychrome $140.00 – 225.00

EP-RI1. 5". No mark. *Animated conundrums.* **Red outline.**

EP-RI2. 6". No mark. *Animated conundrums.* **Same as EP-RI1 except for size and color.**

EP-RI3. 6". No mark. *2 Why is this geometrical fishing?*

EP-RI4. 6". No mark. *4 Why is the poor little rabbit terrified & frightened?*

EP-RI5. 6". No mark. *5 Why would this pastry cook make a good soldier?*

EP-RI6. 6". No mark. *6 What fruit does our sketch represent?*

EP-RI7. 7". No mark. *4 Why are these boys wrong in their arithmetic?*

EP-RI8. 6". No mark. *Pray tell us ladies....*

EP-RI9. 6". No mark. *Riddle — I ever live....*

EP-RI10. 7¼". No mark. *Tis true I have....*

These plates illustrate the story, written in 1719, which pleased "instantly and eternally." Most of these were beautifully made by Brownhills Pottery and are total transfer.

Monochrome $125.00 – 140.00

Polychrome $140.00 – 250.00

EP-RC1. 4³/₄" saucer. Manufactured for H.C. Edmiston, England. *Crusoe making a boat.*

EP-RC2. 6". England, Rd No 69963, B.P. Co. *Crusoe making a boat.*

EP-RC3. 6". England, Rd No 69963, B.P. Co. *Crusoe teaching Friday.*

EP-RC4. 6". Same as EP-RC3 except for color.

EP-RC5. 6". Same as EP-RC3 and 4 except for color.

EP-RC6. 8". Rd No 69963, B.P. Co. *Crusoe finding the foot prints.*

EP-RC7. 7¹/₄". Rd No 69963, B.P. Co. *Crusoe rescues Friday.*

EP-RC8. 7¹/₄". Rd No 69963, B.P. Co. *Crusoe viewing the island.*

EP-RC9. 7¹/₄". No mark. *Robinson Crusoe taking a survey of the island.*

EP-RC10. 8¹/₄". England, Rd No 69963, B.P. Co.
Crusoe at work.

EP-RC11. 8¹/₄". England, Rd No 69963, B.P. Co.
Crusoe on the raft.

EP-RC12. 8". England, Rd No 69963, B.P. Co. *Crusoe and his pets.*

All the plates in this category were made by the same pottery; H. Aynsley & Co., Longton, England, Rd No 426673, about 1904. The standard alphabet is embossed around the rim, and an illustration, encircled by the entire sign language alphabet, is transferred in the center. The signs for "good" and "bad" are between the signs for A and Z. Apparently few of these plates were made; they are seldom seen and quite expensive.

Monochrome $185.00 – 225.00

Polychrome $225.00 – 400.00

EP-SL1. 6". H. Aynsley & Co., Longton, England. Cats shaking hands.

EP-SL2. 8". Marked as above. Same as EP-SL1 except for size and color.

EP-SL3. 8¹/₄". Marked as above. Two Dutch children with duck along a wall.

EP-SL4. 8¹/₄". Maked as above. Boy kissing girl; another child looks on.

This category includes baseball, cricket, rugby, horse racing (including steeplechase), and fishing. We included adult sports only, leaving children's sports under CHILDREN AT PLAY.

Monochrome $135.00 – 160.00

Polychrome $160.00 – 350.00

EP-S1. 6". No mark. *Harry baiting....*

EP-S2. 6¹/₂". C.A. & Sons, England. Steeple-chase.

EP-S3. 7¹/₂". No mark. Fencing.

EP-S4. 6³/₄". C.A. & Sons, England. Rugby.

EP-S5. 7¹/₄". No mark. *American Sports — out on the third base.*

EP-S6. 6¹/₂". Staffordshire, England. Two horses at wall.

EP-S7. 6³/₄". C.A. & Sons, England. Cricket.

EP-S8. 7¹/₂". C.Λ. & Sons, England. Same as EP S7 except for size and color.

EP-S9. 6³/₄". C.A. & Sons, England. Horse race.

EP-S10. 7¹/₂". C.A. & Sons, England. Same as EP-S9 except for size and color.

ENGLISH STAFFORDSHIRE MUGS

This category, soft paste mugs, is a very attractive and charming one, but collecting it is a real challenge. Mugs, with their delicate and protruding handles, have a much lower survival rate than plates. These handles were attached in a separate operation, and many show exquisite care in their design and manufacture. Some are footed in a fleur-de-lis shape, while others have a stripe of color highlighting them.

The mug dates from an era before the saucer was in use. Mugs are cylindrical, with a thick wall and, sometimes, a re-enforcing band at the base; cups are usually much thinner walled and delicate, and have tapered sides.

In about half of the mug examples extant, the entire alphabet is transferred around the outside surface. In the others, one, two, or three consecutive letters appear, with transfer illustrations. English ABC mugs always used the transfer method.

Sometimes the initial letter is used to begin a short verse, the subject of the illustration; other mugs have just a letter, capital and lower case, perhaps, with illustration. Often the skill (or lack thereof) of the artist made identifying the drawing a real challenge, even when the first letter of the object is known.

Fewer mugs than plates have manufacturers' marks; fewer still have the British Registry diamond.

The scarcity of Staffordshire mugs, plus their charm, make them among the most expensive categories to collect.

Values are listed with each piece, but any *old* perfect English ABC mug is worth at least $110.00. Monochrome mugs usually are worth less than polychrome, but some single color mugs are very old, adding $50 to the value. Crusoe B.P. Co. mugs are also very expensive.

Newer English ABC mugs are also included in this list.

Animals, wild and domestic, are well represented in this mug category. We suppose children learned their alphabet more quickly when they could match a letter with an animal they recognized. A most charming category.

Values with each piece.

EM-A1. 2³/₄". No mark. K, L. *K is a kitten..., L is a ladder....* $150.00 – 200.00.

EM-A2. 2³/₄". No mark. C, D. Cat and dog. $150.00 – 180.00.

EM-A3. 2¹/₂". No mark. E, F. *E is for elephant..., F is for fox....* $150.00 – 200.00.

EM-A4. 2³/₄". No mark. F. Fox. $130.00 – 150.00.

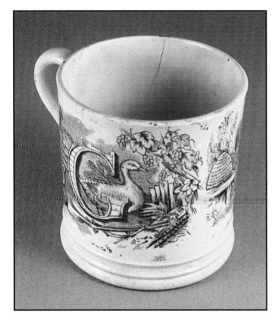

EM-A5. 2³/₄". No mark. G, H. Goose and horse. $150.00 – 180.00.

EM-A6. 2¹/₂". No mark. C, D. *C begins cat..., D is for dash....* $125.00 –150.00.

EM-A7. 2³/₄". Adams, England. C, D. *C is for cat..., D for donkey....* $150.00 – 180.00.

EM-A8. 2¹/₂". Not old. Lord Nelson Pottery, England. Rabbit. $30.00 – 40.00.

EM-A9. 2¹/₂". No mark. E, F. Eagle and Fanny outside. C, D. Cow and Dandy inside cup. Rare. $175.00 – 220.00.

EM-A10. 2³/₄". Allertons, England. A–Z. Dog and rabbit. $130.00 – 150.00.

EM-A11. 2¹/₂". No mark. A–Z around rim. *Rabbits.* $150.00 – 175.00.

EM-A12. 3". No mark. L. *Landseers Dog Parliment.* $200.00 – 225.00.

A rather sparse, but very desireable, group of mugs. This is one of the smallest mug categories; bird mugs are seldom seen for sale.

Values with each piece.

EM-B1. 2³/₄". Allertons, England. A–Z. Rooster and goat. $160.00 – 180.00.

EM-B2. 2³/₄". A. Shaw & Son, Mersey Pottery, Burslem, England. A–Z. *Kingfisher*. $160.00 – 225.00.

EM-B3. 2³/₄". A. Shaw & Son, Mersey Pottery, Burslem, England. A–Z. Bird. $150.00 – 225.00.

EM-B4. 2³/₄". No mark. V. Vulture. $110.00 – 150.00.

There are almost as many mugs with children featured as plates. We think this is because children of the period could easily identify with the illustrations.

Values with each piece.

EM-C1. 2³/₄". Staffordshire, England. S, T, U. *Going to school.* $160.00 – 220.00.

EM-C2. 2³/₄". No mark. D, E, F. Girl selling flowers to gentlemen. $150.00 – 175.00.

EM-C3. 2³/₄". No mark. A, B, C. Child with dog. This mug was part of a set with EM-C2. $150.00 – 175.00.

EM-C4. 2³/₄". Staffordshire, England. V, W, X. Boy getting spanked. $150.00 – 190.00.

EM-C5. 2¹/₂". Staffordshire, England. V, W, X. Children on see-saw. $150.00 – 175.00.

EM-C6. 2³/₄". Staffordshire, England. D, E, F. *Shuttlecock.* $150.00 – 175.00.

EM-C7. 2³/₄". No mark. P, Q, R. *Kite flying.* $150.00 – 200.00.

EM-C8. 2³/₄". **Staffordshire, England. A, B, C.** *Blind-man's bluff.* $140.00 – 175.00.

EM-C9. 2³/₄". **No mark. G, H, I. Girl and tree.** $130.00 – 165.00.

EM-C10. 2³/₄". **No mark. M, N, O.** *Whip-top.* $150.00 – 200.00.

There are far fewer mugs in this category than there are plates on the same subject. Children's rhymes and stories must have been an extremely popular theme, and we think that a large number of mugs must have been made, used, and therefore broken. Mugs on this subject are almost as scarce as birds.

Values with each piece.

EM-CRS1. 2¹/₂". Rd No 69963, B.P. Co. A–Z *Crusoe teaching Friday.* $200.00 – 250.00.

EM-CRS2. 2". No mark. A–Z. *Crusoe at work.* $150.00 – 175.00.

EM-CRS3. 2". No mark. A–Z. *Whittington and his cat.* $130.00 – 165.00.

EM-CRS4. 2³/₄". No mark. Little Jack Horner. $150.00 – 200.00.

EM-CRS5. 2³/₄". No mark. A–V embossed around rim. *Grandmamma's Tales. Hush-a-bye baby....* $150.00 – 180.00.

EM-CRS6. 2¹/₂". Wood and Sons, England. A, B, C. *Ride a cock horse....* Not old. $30.00 – 40.00.

There are a relatively large number of mugs in this category. Letters, capital and sometimes lower case, are prominently featured, with descriptive illustrations.

Values with each piece.

EM-L1. 2³/₄". No mark. Y. Youth. $150.00 – 170.00.

EM-L2. 2³/₄". No mark. X. A variation of EM-L11. $130.00 – 150.00.

EM-L3. 2³/₄". No mark. A apple, B ball. $150.00 – 175.00.

EM-L4. 2³/₄". No mark. L, R. Ladder and rabbit. $130.00 – 165.00.

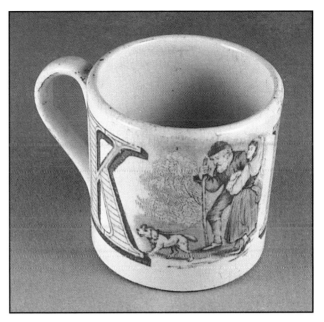

EM-L5. 2¹/₂". No mark. K, L. Man with woman and dog. $200.00 – 230.00.

EM-L6. 2¹/₂". No mark. C, D. Child and devotion. $130.00 – 160.00.

EM-L7. 2³/₄". No mark. S, T. Study and teach. $150.00 – 175.00.

EM-L8. 2⁵/₈". No mark. H. *Shepherd's crook.* $175.00 – 200.00.

EM-L9. 2¹/₂". No mark. U, V. U umpire (magistrate in wig), V volume. $120.00 – 150.00.

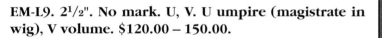

EM-L10. 2³/₄". No mark. N. $120.00 – 150.00.

EM-L11. 2³/₄". No mark. X. A variation of EM-L2. $130.00 – 150.00.

EM-L12. 2³/₄". No mark. U. *Uncle.* $150.00 – 170.00.

EM-L13. 2¹/₂". No mark. E, F. *E was an Esquire...,* F *was a farm....* $140.00 – 200.00.

A popular subject in Victorian England, but for some reason many more plates exist with a religious motif than mugs.

Values with each piece.

EM-R1. 2". No mark. A–Z. *Eligah fed by the ravens.* $150.00 – 175.00.

EM-R2. 2³/₄". No mark. W, X. *Widow & X is the cross.* $130.00 – 160.00.

EM-R3. 2¹/₂". No mark. O, P. *Obadia and Peter.* $130.00 – 150.00.

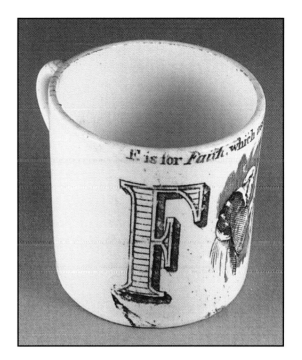

EM-R4. 2³/₄". No mark. *F is for faith.* $120.00 – 150.00.

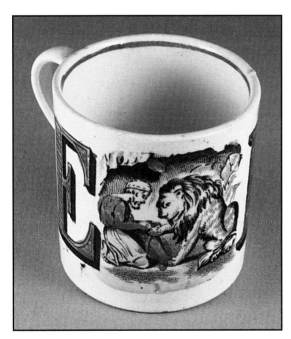

EM-R5. 2³/₄". No mark. E, F. Bible scenes. $150.00 – 175.00.

EM-R6. 2¹/₂". No mark. A-Z embossed faintly around rim. *Search the Scriptures.* $130.00 – 160.00.

Here are the mugs which wouldn't quite fit in any other category. A very attractive, albeit small, group of mugs.

Values with each piece.

EM-S1. 3". No mark. A–Z. Children playing. $130.00 – 165.00.

EM-S2. 2³/4". No mark. A–Z. Girl, cow, house on hill. $130.00 – 175.00.

EM-S3. 2³/₄". England, British Registry mark. A Z. Seashore scene with man. $150.00 – 175.00.

EM-S4. 2³/₄". No mark. A–Z. Seashore scene. $150.00 – 185.00.

EM-S5. 2³/₄". No mark. A–Z. Children playing. Same as EM-S1 except for size and color. $130.00 – 165.00.

As stated earlier in this book, sets of any kind are scarce. We have a few "almost" sets: mugs EM-CRS2, EM-CRS3, and EM-R1 are almost a match with EP-CRS14 and EP-CRS15, and EP-RC1 through EP-RC5. We're sure these patterns of cup, saucer, and plate were made in matching sets, but we've never seen such a set. Also, color must have varied day to day at the potteries as one batch of color ran out and a new one was mixed, which added a new variable to the mix. There are a few shades of blue, for instance, which we're sure was inadvertent.

Indeed, English sets are so hard to find, it's difficult to assign a value to them. The following is an educated guesstimate.

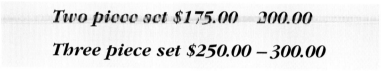

Two piece set $175.00 – 200.00

Three piece set $250.00 – 300.00

ES-1. 2¹/₂" high mug. James Kent, Old Foley, Made in England. *Jack and Jill....* **1950s. $50.00 – 60.00.**

Although yellow ware was manufactured in various countries, including the U.S.A., we are sure this plate is English because it has three indents (for rack drying) which are peculiar to English plates.

Value is listed with piece.

EP-YELO1. 8". No mark. Yellow ware divided dish with alphabet around rim. $40.00 – 50.00.

GERMAN HARD PASTE ABC WARE

The manufacture of ABC plates and cups in Germany began much later than in England, around 1890. German hard paste china is thinner and whiter than Staffordshire. It offers the collector fewer choices than soft paste ware, although enough variety exists to build a very attractive collection of German ABC ware alone.

Here, the transfer method of illustration was not used. Instead, a decal was applied to the ware. These decals are in full color and used the same method of chromolithography found on postcards of the period. Of course, since the decals were mechanically reproduced, the German china of a specific pattern has a cookie-cutter sameness, unlike the handmade English product.

The alphabet was usually embossed and sometimes embellished with gilt. The decal subjects included chickens, cats, and other animals, and sometimes featured people.

$75.00 – 130.00

GP-1. 7". No mark. *Buster Brown.*

GP-2. 7". No mark. Cat and child, horse, chariot.

GP-3. 7". No mark. Three girls with fan.

GP-4. 7". No mark. Green with animals around rim.

GP-5. 7". No mark. Cats playing cards at table.

GP-6. 6". No mark. Flowers in center, yellow luster rim.

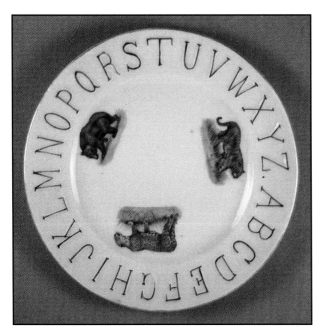

GP-7. 6¼". No mark. Bear, tiger, and leopard.

GP-8. 7". No mark. Cats with fowl on platter, flowers around.

GP-9. 6". No mark. Girl, boy, dog planting tree.

GP-10. 7". No mark. Two girls with fans.

GP-11. 6". No mark. Girl with dog and puppy.

GP-12. 7". No mark. Pink luster, girl with two puppies in basket.

GP-13. 7". No mark. Pink luster. Girls playing Ring around the Rosie.

GP-14. 6". No mark. Gold alphabet with three chickens.

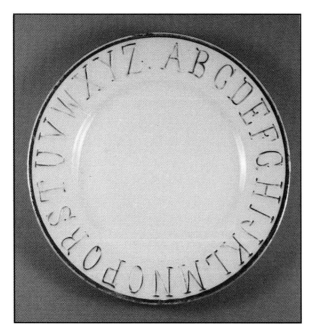

GP-15. 7". Germany. Gold alphabet.

GP-16. 7". No mark. Cats in rowboat.

GP-17. 7". No mark. _Merry Christmas._

GP-18. 7". No mark. Three girls and flowers.

GP-19. 7". No mark. Similar to GP-8 but without flowers.

GP-20. 6". No mark. Two children, bubbles, dog, cat, and dolls.

GP-21. 7". No mark. Rooster and hen.

GP-22. 6". No mark. Two circus horses with rider.

GP-23. 7". No mark. Three children, goat pulling cart.

GP-24. 7". No mark. Pink luster. Two Dutch girls.

GP-25. 7". No mark. Two girls in bonnets and flowers.

GP-26. 6". No mark. Elephants on parade.

GP-27. 6¼". No mark. Bird, horn, saw, hammer.

GP-28. 7". No mark. Boy kissing girl, another girl objects.

GP-29. 7". No mark. Cat and dog in creamer.

GP-30. 7". No mark. Cats pulling a chariot.

GP-31. 6¼". No mark. *View of Penn Park, York, Pa.*

GP-32. 7¹/₂". No mark. Girl and dolls getting portrait taken.

GP-33. 6". No mark. *This is the house that Jack built.*

GP-34. 6". No mark. Floral pattern.

Generally, cups and matching saucers are purchased together, so we have listed them as such. However, variety is limited in this category. If one purchases a cup by itself, it is likely that a matching saucer and even a plate will turn up later. We have, accordingly, listed values separately.

Many cups and saucers were decorated like the German plates, with decal illustrations and gilt-accented embossed alphabet. Sometimes the saucer contained the complete alphabet, but the letters appeared larger on the cup and the manufacturer ran out of cup before he ran out of alphabet.

Decoration varies widely on the saucers. The alphabet, gilted or plain, and/or full-color decals, or plain gold trim make the saucers every bit as colorful as the cups and plates. Almost any combination of cups and saucers go together.

Cup and saucer $65.00 – 80.00

Cup alone $50.00 – 60.00

Saucer alone $6.00 – 10.00

GCS-1. 2¹/₂". No mark. Pink luster. A–Z on both.

GCS-2. 2¹/₂". Made in Germany. A–K on cup. Fruits, boy, dog.

GCS-3. 2¹/₂". No mark. A–L on cup. Tiger, elephant.

GCS-4. 2¹/₂". Germany. A–L on cup. White with gold lettering and trim.

GCS-5. 2¹/₂". Germany. A–L on cup. Rooster, hens, chicks.

GCS-6. 2¹/₂". Germany. A–Z on cup. Green, plain saucer.

Mugs are made with straight sides, for use without a saucer. German ABC mugs are decorated like the cups, with decals and/or gilt-decorated embossed alphabet.

$65.00 – 75.00

GM-1. 2³/₄". Germany 108. A–L, embossed.

GM-2. 2¹/₂". Bavaria, J. Rieber Co. A–Z embossed. Boy reading book, ducks.

GM-3. 2⁷/₈". No mark. A–Z. Pink floral decal.

German ABC china, being manufactured in but a limited variety, may be purchased by the piece, with the collector usually able to build and complete a set later. Of course, it's always better to buy the complete set in the first place, but since German cups, saucers, and plates do not vary much in color and motif, there is little chance of ending up with an incomplete set.

$165.00 – 185.00

GS-1. 2¹/₂". Made in Germany. A–Z on cup, saucer, and plate. Green with chickens.

GS-2. 2¹/₂". No mark. Same as GS-1 except entire set is pink.

GS-3. 3¹/₂". Three Crown China, Germany. Creamer, bowl, plate. Pale orange accent.

GS-4. 3¹/₂". Three Crown China, Germany. Same as GS-3 but purple accent.

Tin ware (actually sheet iron plated with tin) can be very old. The plates pictured in this category date, in come cases, from before the American Civil War. The plates were made in both America and England, but since none of these pieces bear identifying marks, the country of origin can be deduced from the plate's subject matter.

Aluminum ABC plates are included here, also. They date from the 1920s and are shown in a few of our mail-order catalogs from that period.

Tin plates, while limited in variety compared with some of the other categories, have been getting very popular with collectors, and prices continue to rise.

☀ *PLATES* ☀

Values are listed with each piece.

TP-1. 8". No mark. *Her Majesty Queen Victoria.* $300.00 – 400.00.

TP-2. 7³/₄". No mark. *Mary had a little lamb....* $130.00 – 160.00.

TP-3. 7³/₄". No mark. *Who killed cock robin....* $130.00 – 150.00.

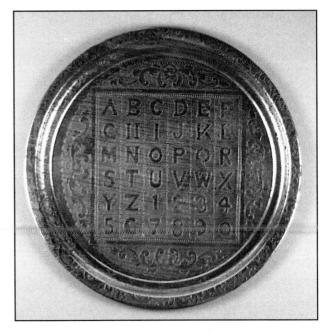

TP-4. 8". No mark. *A, B, C....* $80.00 – 100.00.

TP-5. 8³/₄". No mark. *Hi diddle diddle....* $80.00 – 100.00.

TP-6. 6¹/₄". No mark. Alphabet around rim. $60.00 – 95.00.

TP-7. 5¹/₂". No mark. Horse. $160.00 – 220.00.

TP-8. 5¹/₂". No mark. *Jumbo*. $100.00 – 160.00.

TP-9. 6". No mark. *Washington*. $175.00 – 200.00.

TP-10. 6". Tudor Plate Oneida Community. *Simple Simon....* $65.00 – 95.00.

TP-11. 5½". No mark. *Liberty.* $110.00 – 150.00.

TP-12. 4½". No mark. Alphabet around rim. $65.00 – 95.00.

TP-13. 4¼". No mark. *Victoria & Albert.* $300.00 – 450.00.

TP-14. 2¾". No mark. Alphabet around rim. $65.00 – 100.00.

TP-15. 3". No mark. **Girl and boy with hoop.** $165.00 – 225.00.

TP-16. 3". No mark. *General Tom Thumb.* $200.00 – 300.00.

TP-17. 6". No mark. **Aluminum deep dish.** $15.00 – 25.00.

TP-18. 7½". No mark. **Aluminum deep dish.** $10.00 – 20.00.

TP-19. 7". No mark. Aluminum, alphabet around rim. $10.00 – 20.00.

TP-20. 2⁷/₈". No mark. Lion. $300.00.

TP-21. 8". No mark. Agateware. Alphabet with clock face. $250.00 – 275.00.

These are actually mugs because they come without saucers and have a cylindrical shape, but "tin cup" is part of our language.

Variety is rather limited. Each piece was soldered by hand from pieces of stamped tin-plated iron. Other information on each piece is included in the caption.

Prices for this ware continue to rise, in part because the ABC collector is competing with the tin ware collector.

Variety is limited so values are listed with each piece.

TC-1. 1⁷/₈" high. No mark. Blue mercuric compound coating, poisonous. About 1860. $250.00 – 275.00.

TC-2. 1⁷/₈" high. No mark. Tin plated, worn. $150.00 – 175.00.

TC-3. 1⁵/₈" high. No mark. Tin plated. Same as TC-2 but smaller. The same die was used to form the decoration as TC-2, this same die was also used on the "growler" TM-2. $150.00 – 175.00.

TC-4. 2¹/₂" high. Forbes Silver Co., USA. Silverplated mug. $65.00 – 75.00.

This category covers all tin or metal ABC which doesn't fit anywhere else.

Values with each piece.

TM-1. 5³/4" long. No mark. *For a good child.* **Rattle with whistle in handle (not working). $125.00 – 150.00.**

TM-2. 2" high. No mark. Lunch kettle with lid (growler). $200.00 – 250.00.

TM-3. 3" high. Leonard Silverplate, Italy. Coin bank. $25.00 – 30.00.

⚞ *LITHO AND OTHER ABC WARE* ⚟

We decided to give litho ware its own category because it was made much later than the plain tin ware and is printed in colors.

Regarding LAVA plates—the LAVA name dates from 1897 and is now owned by the Block Drug Company, who purchased it from Proctor and Gamble in 1995. A letter to Proctor and Gamble's Corporate Archives brought the response that they think the litho LAVA plates date from about 1900.

There is much less variety in litho so approximate values are listed with each piece.

⚞ *PLATES* ⚟

LP-1. 6". No mark. Alphabet around rim, numerals in center. $110.00 – 125.00.

LP-2. 6". Made in U.S.A. Girls chasing butterflies. $110.00 – 150.00.

LP-3. 6". Ohio Art Co., Bryan, O., U.S.A. Two cats with yarn basket. Also found in 4¼". $65.00 – 110.00.

LP-4. 6¼". Made in Bryan, O., U.S.A. Girl on swing. Also found in 3½". $65.00 – 110.00.

LP-5. 7¾". No mark. Peter Rabbit. $200.00 – 350.00.

LP-6. 6¼". LAVA (Lava Soap Co.). *Tom the piper's son....* $85.00 – 125.00.

LP-7. 6". LAVA. *Jack and Jill....* **$85.00 – 125.00.**

LP-8. 6". Kemp Manufacturing Co., Toronto. *After supper run a mile.* **$150.00 – 200.00.**

LP-9. 6". LAVA. *Here we go round....* **$65.00 – 110.00.**

As stated earlier in this book, sets, of any kind, are scarce. The sets below, if complete, would sell for at least $500.00, and be well worth it.

LS-1. 1¹/₂" high cups with saucers, small and large plates with alphabet. Cats. $175.00 incomplete.

LS-2. 2" high cup with ABC saucer, ABC plate, coffeepot with lid. Girl on swing. $175.00 incomplete.

This category covers lithographed tin ware, some of which may have been made quite recently.

Values with each piece.

LM-1. 7¹/₄". Chein, Made in USA. Sand sifter, about 1950. $50.00 – 60.00.

LM-2. 6" long. TINDECO. Candy container with lid. 1920s. $120.00 – 130.00.

LM-3. 2¹/₄" high. No mark. Litho mug. *A good girl* with entire alphabet. $125.00 – 150.00.

Our native product, while manufactured much later than the English, is interesting and varied enough to merit its own category.

Many of the plates were advertising giveaways with business names on either the front or back of the plate.

⚛ *PLATES* ⚛

$75.00 – 135.00

AP-1. 7". Smith Phillips. Sunbonnet girls making a pie crust.

AP-2. 7". No mark. *Baby Bunting runs away....*

AP-3. 8". No mark. Similar to AP-2.

AP-4. 7¹/₄". No mark. *Baby Bunting and her little dog....*

AP-5. 7". No mark. *Baby Bunting while....*

AP-6. 7". D.E. McNicol, East Liverpool, Ohio. *Baby Bunting lifts....*

AP-7. 8". E.L.P. Co. Three rabbits.

AP-8. 6¹/₂". Smith Phillips Porcelain. Bears playing ball.

AP-9. 7". W.E.P. Co. Blueish cat's head with blue letters.

AP-10. 6³/₄". W.E.P. Co. Similar to AP-9 but orange cat.

AP-11. 8¹/₂". No mark. *Little Bo-Peep.*

AP-12. 7¹/₄". No mark. Rabbit in toy car, chick with flag.

AP-13. 7¹/₄". No mark. Gold stamped lettering.

AP-14. 6¹/₂". No mark. Boy and girl with cat, rake.

AP-15. 6¹/₂". No mark. _Jack & Jill._

AP-16. 8". No mark. Two girls with dolls and toys.

AP-17. 8". D.E. McNicol. Advertising giveaway. Roses in center. (M.D. Pennington went out of business about 1950).

AP-18. 6¼". No mark. Braille characters under alphabet. $65.00 – 75.00.

All of these plates are marked HOTEL on the back in black. They are ironstone, very thick and sturdy, and were made to withstand rough handling by dishwashers in hotels, restaurants, cafeterias, etc. All of the plates listed here were made by the Harker Pottery Company, East Liverpool, Ohio, between 1890 and 1920.

Illustrations on the Harker HOTEL backstamped plates are decals which were purchased from one or more commercial decal providers who supplied the industry. Whether decals and advertising were applied to these plates by Harker or by china decorating companies operating nearby is unknown. The Harker Pottery Company was in business from 1840 until 1972.

(For the above information on Harker, the authors are obliged to Harker experts, Donna and Bill Gray of Columbia, MD).

$75.00 – 135.00

**AP-HOTEL-1. 6". HOTEL. *Thoroughbreds.*
Sepia print.**

AP-HOTEL-2. 6¼". HOTEL. *Little Boy Blue.*

AP-HOTEL-3. 6". HOTEL. *Memories.*

AP-HOTEL-4. 6". HOTEL. *Dolly's sail.*

AP-HOTEL-5. 7". HOTEL. Horse's head. Sepia print.

AP-HOTEL-6. 6". HOTEL. *The sick puppy.*

AP-HOTEL-7. 6". HOTEL. Blue bird.

AP-HOTEL-8. 6¹/4". HOTEL. Birds, king, and pie.

🔻 *MISCELLANEOUS* 🔻

We have been unable to locate much in the way of American ABC material except for plates.

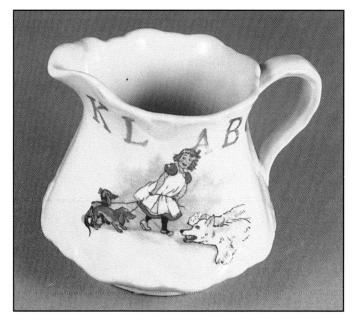

AM-1. 3" high creamer. Potters' Co-Operative Co. Semi Vitreous. 1920s. Probably part of a set. $60.00 – 75.00.

⚐ *GLASS ABC WARE* ⚐

Because glassware of any kind is easily reproduced, collectors are understandably a little wary about investing in glass ABC ware. We have no definitive proof that reproductions of the plates illustrated below exist, as far as we know, all of these are original and old.

We have included an old chalksware ABC "plate" because it almost exactly duplicates plates GLP-11, 12, and 13. According to *Schroeder's Antiques Price Guide*, chalkware, a form of folk art, was made from 1860 until 1890 and often sold door to door.

Also in this section are mugs from about 1900.

⚐ *PLATES* ⚐

Values with each piece.

GLP-1. Two dishes from an ice cream set. Small dish with alphabet 2³/₄". Platter, no alphabet, 5¹/₂". No mark. Plate $50.00, platter $40.00. The complete set consists of six plates with platter. Sets are valued at $500.00.

GLP-2. 7". No mark. Months, days, clock face, alphabet. $50.00 – 60.00.

GLP-3. 7". No mark. Alphabet, numerals, clock face. $50.00 – 60.00.

GLP-4. 6". No mark. *Christmas Eve.*
$175.00 – 200.00.

GLP-5. 6¼". No mark. Diamond center design. $50.00 – 60.00.

GLP-6. 6". No mark. Rooster. $65.00 – 75.00.

GLP-7. 6". No mark. Fan pattern. $65.00 – 75.00.

GLP-8. 6". No mark. *Sancho Panza & Dapple.* **$50.00 – 60.00.**

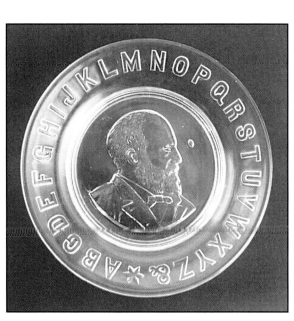

GLP-9. 6". No mark. President Garfield. $125.00 – 150.00.

GLP-10. 6". No mark. Ducks, yellow glass. $60.00 – 70.00.

GLP-11. 8". No mark. Vaseline glass. Child's face (Emma) $30.00.

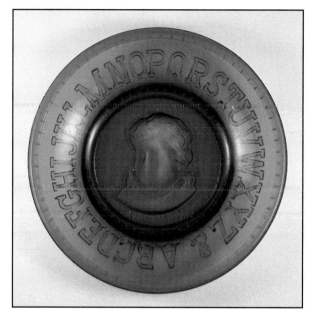

GLP-12. 8". Same as GLP-11 except orange. $30.00.

GLP-13. 8". Same as GLP-11 except blue. $30.00.

GLP-14. 7¹/₂". No mark. Carnival glass. $90.00 – 120.00.

GLP-15. 7". No mark. Milk glass. $50.00 – 60.00.

GLP-16. 6¹/₂". No mark. *Xmas 1890*. Chalkware. Same design as *Emma* plates GLP-11, 12, and 13. $50.00 – 70.00.

GLP-17. 2³/₄" high. No mark. Glass ABC Mug. Three panels, about 1900. $85.00 – 100.00.

GLP-18. 3". No mark. A–Z. Milk glass mug. $65.00 – 85.00.

COLLECTOR BOOKS

I n f o r m i n g   T o d a y ' s   C o l l e c t o r

*For over two decades we have been keeping collectors informed
on trends and values in all fields of antiques and collectibles.*

BOOKS ON GLASS AND POTTERY

1810	American Art Glass, Shuman	$29.95
1312	Blue & White Stoneware, McNerney	$9.95
1959	Blue Willow, 2nd Ed., Gaston	$14.95
4553	Coll. Glassware from the 40's, 50's, 60's, 3rd Ed., Florence	$19.95
3816	Collectible Vernon Kilns, Nelson	$24.95
3311	Collecting Yellow Ware – Id. & Value Gd., McAllister	$16.95
1373	Collector's Ency. of American Dinnerware, Cunningham	$24.95
3815	Coll. Ency. of Blue Ridge Dinnerware, Newbound	$19.95
2272	Collector's Ency. of California Pottery, Chipman	$24.95
3811	Collector's Ency. of Colorado Pottery, Carlton	$24.95
3312	Collector's Ency. of Children's Dishes, Whitmyer	$19.95
2133	Collector's Ency. of Cookie Jars, Roerig	$24.95
3723	Coll. Ency. of Cookie Jars-Volume II, Roerig	$24.95
4552	Collector's Ency. of Depression Glass, 12th Ed., Florence	$19.95
2209	Collector's Ency. of Fiesta, 7th Ed., Huxford	$19.95
1439	Collector's Ency. of Flow Blue China, Gaston	$19.95
3812	Coll. Ency. of Flow Blue China, 2nd Ed., Gaston	$24.95
3813	Collector's Ency. of Hall China, 2nd Ed., Whitmyer	$24.95
2334	Collector's Ency. of Majolica Pottery, Katz-Marks	$19.95
1358	Collector's Ency. of McCoy Pottery, Huxford	$19.95
3313	Collector's Ency. of Niloak, Gifford	$19.95
3837	Collector's Ency. of Nippon Porcelain I, Van Patten	$24.95
2089	Collector's Ency. of Nippon Porcelain II, Van Patten	$24.95
1665	Collector's Ency. of Nippon Porcelain III, Van Patten	$24.95
4712	Collector's Ency. of Nippon Porcelain IV, Van Patten	$24.95
1447	Collector's Ency. of Noritake, 1st Series, Van Patten	$19.95
1034	Collector's Ency. of Roseville Pottery, Huxford	$19.95
1035	Collector's Ency. of Roseville Pottery, 2nd Ed., Huxford	$19.95
3314	Collector's Ency. of Van Briggle Art Pottery, Sasicki	$24.95
2339	Collector's Guide to Shawnee Pottery, Vanderbilt	$19.95
1425	Cookie Jars, Westfall	$9.95
3440	Cookie Jars, Book II, Westfall	$19.95
2275	Czechoslovakian Glass & Collectibles, Barta	$16.95
4716	Elegant Glassware of the Depression Era, 7th Ed., Florence	$19.95
3725	Fostoria - Pressed, Blown & Hand Molded Shapes, Kerr	$24.95
3883	Fostoria Stemware - The Crystal for America, Long	$24.95
3886	Kitchen Glassware of the Depression Years, 5th Ed., Florence	$19.95
4772	McCoy Pottery, Coll. Reference & Value Guide, Hanson	$19.95
4725	Pocket Guide to Depression Glass, 10th Ed., Florence	$9.95
3825	Puritan Pottery, Morris	$24.95
1670	Red Wing Collectibles, DePasquale	$9.95
1440	Red Wing Stoneware, DePasquale	$9.95
1958	So. Potteries Blue Ridge Dinnerware, 3rd Ed., Newbound	$14.95
4634	Standard Carnival Glass, 5th Ed., Edwards	$24.95
3327	Watt Pottery – Identification & Value Guide, Morris	$19.95
2224	World of Salt Shakers, 2nd Ed., Lechner	$24.95

BOOKS ON DOLLS & TOYS

4707	A Decade of Barbie Dolls and Collectibles, 1981 - 1991, Summers	$19.95
2079	Barbie Fashion, Vol. 1, 1959-1967, Eames	$24.95
3310	Black Dolls – 1820 - 1991 – Id. & Value Guide, Perkins	$17.95
1529	Collector's Ency. of Barbie Dolls, DeWein	$19.95
2338	Collector's Ency. of Disneyana, Longest & Stern	$24.95
3727	Coll. Guide to Ideal Dolls, Izen	$18.95

4645	Madame Alexander Price Guide #21, Smith	$9.95
4723	Matchbox Toys, 1947 to 1996, Johnson	$18.95
4647	Modern Collector's Dolls, 8th series, Smith	$24.95
1540	Modern Toys, 1930 - 1980, Baker	$19.95
4640	Patricia Smith's Doll Values – Antique to Modern, 12th ed.	$12.95
4728	Schroeder's Coll. Toys, 3rd Edition	$17.95
3826	Story of Barbie, Westenhouser, No Values	$19.95
2028	Toys, Antique & Collectible, Longest	$14.95
1808	Wonder of Barbie, Manos	$9.95
1430	World of Barbie Dolls, Manos	$9.95

OTHER COLLECTIBLES

1457	American Oak Furniture, McNerney	$9.95
3716	American Oak Furniture, Book II, McNerney	$12.95
4704	Antique & Collectible Buttons, Wisniewski	$19.95
2333	Antique & Collectible Marbles, 3rd Ed., Grist	$9.95
1748	Antique Purses, Holiner	$19.95
1426	Arrowheads & Projectile Points, Hothem	$7.95
1278	Art Nouveau & Art Deco Jewelry, Baker	$9.95
1714	Black Collectibles, Gibbs	$19.95
4708	B.J. Summers' Guide to Coca-Cola, Summers	$19.95
1128	Bottle Pricing Guide, 3rd Ed., Cleveland	$7.95
3717	Christmas Collectibles, 2nd Ed., Whitmyer	$24.95
1752	Christmas Ornaments, Johnson	$19.95
3718	Collectible Aluminum, Grist	$16.95
2132	Collector's Ency. of American Furniture, Vol. I, Swedberg	$24.95
2271	Collector's Ency. of American Furniture, Vol. II, Swedberg	$24.95
3720	Coll. Ency. of American Furniture, Vol III, Swedberg	$24.95
3722	Coll. Ency. of Compacts, Carryalls & Face Powder Boxes, Mueller	$24.95
2018	Collector's Ency. of Granite Ware, Greguire	$24.95
3430	Coll. Ency. of Granite Ware, Book 2, Greguire	$24.95
1441	Collector's Guide to Post Cards, Wood	$9.95
2276	Decoys, Kangas	$24.95
1716	Fifty Years of Fashion Jewelry, Baker	$19.95
4568	Flea Market Trader, 10th Ed., Huxford	$12.95
3819	General Store Collectibles, Wilson	$24.95
3436	Grist's Big Book of Marbles, Everett Grist	$19.95
2278	Grist's Machine Made & Contemporary Marbles	$9.95
1424	Hatpins & Hatpin Holders, Baker	$9.95
4721	Huxford's Collectible Advertising – Id. & Value Gd., 3rd Ed	$24.95
4648	Huxford's Old Book Value Guide, 8th Ed.	$19.95
1181	100 Years of Collectible Jewelry, Baker	$9.95
2216	Kitchen Antiques – 1790 - 1940, McNerney	$14.95
4724	Modern Guns – Id. & Val. Gd., 11th Ed., Quertermous	$12.95
2026	Railroad Collectibles, 4th Ed., Baker	$14.95
1632	Salt & Pepper Shakers, Guarnaccia	$9.95
1888	Salt & Pepper Shakers II, Guarnaccia	$14.95
2220	Salt & Pepper Shakers III, Guarnaccia	$14.95
3443	Salt & Pepper Shakers IV, Guarnaccia	$18.95
4727	Schroeder's Antiques Price Guide, 15th Ed.	$14.95
4729	Sewing Tools & Trinkets, Thompson	$24.95
2096	Silverplated Flatware, 4th Ed., Hagan	$14.95
2348	20th Century Fashionable Plastic Jewelry, Baker	$19.95
3828	Value Guide to Advertising Memorabilia, Summers	$18.95
3830	Vintage Vanity Bags & Purses, Gerson	$24.95

Schroeder's
ANTIQUES
Price Guide

. . . is the #1 best-selling antiques & collectibles value guide on the market today, and here's why . . .

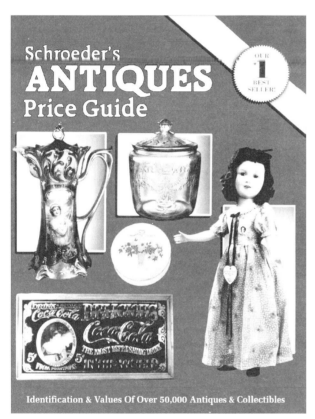

Schroeder's
ANTIQUES
Price Guide

Identification & Values Of Over 50,000 Antiques & Collectibles

8½ x 11, 608 Pages, $12.95

- *More than 300 advisors, well-known dealers, and top-notch collectors work together with our editors to bring you accurate information regarding pricing and identification.*

- *More than 45,000 items in almost 500 categories are listed along with hundreds of sharp original photos that illustrate not only the rare and unusual, but the common, popular collectibles as well.*

- *Each large close-up shot shows important details clearly. Every subject is represented with histories and background information, a feature not found in any of our competitors' publications.*

- *Our editors keep abreast of newly developing trends, often adding several new categories a year as the need arises.*

If it merits the interest of today's collector, you'll find it in *Schroeder's*. And you can feel confident that the information we publish is up to date and accurate. Our advisors thoroughly check each category to spot inconsistencies, listings that may not be entirely reflective of market dealings, and lines too vague to be of merit. Only the best of the lot remains for publication.

Without doubt, you'll find
SCHROEDER'S ANTIQUES PRICE GUIDE
the only one to buy for
reliable information and values.

COLLECTOR BOOKS
A Division of Schroeder Publishing Co., Inc.